■SCHOLASTIC

GRADES K–2

BEST PRACTICES *in Action*

Math Test Prep
That Matters!

50 Standards-Based Math Prompts That Develop
Students' Critical Thinking and Deepen Their
Understanding of Key Math Concepts

JOSEPH A. PORZIO

NEW YORK • TORONTO • LONDON • AUCKLAND • SYDNEY
MEXICO CITY • NEW DELHI • HONG KONG • BUENOS AIRES

Teaching *Resources*

Cover design by Jason Robinson
Interior design by Holly Grundon
Interior illustrations by Rita Lascaro

ISBN-13: 978-0-439-59721-0
ISBN-10: 0-439-59721-8
Copyright © 2006 by Joseph A. Porzio
All rights reserved.
Printed in the USA.

1 2 3 4 5 6 7 8 9 10   31   15 14 13 12 11 10 09 08 07 06

Contents

Introduction

In an age now driven by the relentless necessity
of scientific and technological advance, the current
preparation that students in the United States receive
in mathematics and science is, in a word, unacceptable.

— Thomas L. Friedman, *The World Is Flat:*
A Brief History of the Twenty-First Century

Over the past three decades educators, business leaders, and policymakers calling for education reform have voiced deep concerns over our students' mathematics and science achievement (Clements, Sarama, & DiBiase, 2004). These concerns seem especially justified when we compare our students' scores on international tests, such as Trends in International Mathematics and Science Study (TIMSS), with those of students from other nations. In 2003, U.S. fourth-grade students ranked 12th out of 25 countries in math scores (International Association for the Evaluation of Educational Achievement, TIMSS, 2003).

In 1983, the U.S. Department of Education published the report "A Nation at Risk," often cited as the origin of current reform efforts. GOALS 2000, signed into law on March 31, 1994, listed a series of ambitious goals, which includes making the United States "first in the world in mathematics and science education." Even the National Assessment of Educational Progress (NAEP), the "Nation's Report Card," prompts repeated calls for reform. Just after the start of the new millennium, the federal government, through the No Child Left Behind Act (NCLB), expanded its role in education by establishing accountability and certification requirements that affected students, educators, and public schools across America. In his January 2006 State of the Union address, President George W. Bush announced ". . . an American Competitiveness Initiative to give our nation's children a firm grounding in math and science."

Clearly, there is more attention and recognition of the importance of mathematics (Kilpatrick, Swafford, & Findell, 2001) in a global economy where the vast majority of jobs require more sophisticated skills than jobs in the past required.

How can we—as regional/district leaders, site supervisors of mathematics, math coaches, classroom teachers, support staff in after-school academic intervention services, and parents—respond to the recognized needs in a manner that will lead to greater academic achievement in mathematics for all students?

Scholastic's Best Practices in Action series provides a definitive response to the call for action from those concerned with promoting and supporting challenging and rigorous classroom instructional practices, rooted in scientifically and/or evidence-based research. The series features promising best practices that impact teaching and learning by ensuring alignment between standards, assessment, and instruction. Among its key features is the recognition that clear, well-defined standards (what students are expected to know and be able to do at their grade level) have a positive impact on classroom teachers' instruction and students' learning.

The Mathematical Sciences Education Board's report "Everybody Counts" (1989) states: "We must ensure that tests measure what is of value, not just what is easy to test. If we want students to investigate, explore, and discover, assessment must not measure just mimicry mathematics." Further, the six key principles in the National Council of Teachers of Mathematics (NCTM) *Principles and Standards for School Mathematics* describe specific features of high-quality mathematics education. Educators who know the value of integrating content and process standards are eager to find supportive resources that complement their mathematics program.

Math Test Prep That Matters! fulfills this need and features a collection of challenging activities designed to promote thinking and foster communication through development of mathematical language (process standards) while enhancing mathematical concepts and their related skills (content standards). This book was written in direct response to the increased attention in mathematics, including that in the formative early childhood years where early childhood educators—the foundation builders—are developing students' understanding of mathematical concepts and their related skills. The challenges found in *Math Test Prep That Matters!* provide opportunities for investigations and rigorous activities that are based in content and designed to promote thinking and oral and written communication skills.

What Does It Mean to Be Proficient in Mathematics?

While we have witnessed profound swings during the past years in what it means to be successful in mathematics (e.g., new math, back to basics, NCTM's Agenda for Action which focused on problem solving), we now recognize that math proficiency requires much more than facility in using computational procedures in arithmetic.

In November 2004, the New York State Education Department's Mathematics Standards Committee presented its recommendations to the New York State Board of Regents, based upon numerous references, including *Principles and Standards for School Mathematics* (NCTM, 2000), *Adding It Up: Helping Children Learn Mathematics* (National Research Council, 2001), *Engaging Young Children in Mathematics: Standards for Early Childhood Mathematics Education* (Lawrence Erlbaum Associates, 2004), and *The Math We Need to "Know" and "Do"* (Corwin Press, 2000). The committee recognized that "every teacher of mathematics, whether at the elementary, middle, or high school level, has an individual goal to provide students with the knowledge and understanding of the mathematics necessary to function in a world that is very dependent upon the application of mathematics. Instructionally, this goal translates into three components:

1. Conceptual understanding
2. Procedural fluency
3. Problem solving"

These components are integrally related and need to be taught simultaneously and should be a component of every lesson.

From Research to Practice

How does *Math Test Prep That Matters!* support, complement, and improve student achievement in mathematics in the classroom?

• It promotes the use of promising instructional practices that are rooted in scientifically/ evidence-based research, as defined in the U.S. Department of Education's website at www.ed.gov and its link to the What Works Clearinghouse. (NOTE: On May 15th, 2006, U.S. Secretary of Education Margaret Spellings announced the names of seventeen expert panelists to comprise the National Mathematics Advisory Panel. The panel's findings and determinations in the area of mathematics will serve as a basis for building capacity and proficiency in the area of mathematics.)

• It develops conceptual understanding and their related skills while promoting communication, reasoning, and thinking. Focusing instruction on the meaningful development of important mathematical ideas increases the level of student understanding (Brownell, 1945). There is a long history of research on the effects of teaching for meaning and understanding.

• It provides several opportunities through the graphic prompts for students to invent new knowledge through non-routine problems. Teachers should periodically introduce a lesson involving a new skill by posing it as a problem to be solved and regularly allow students to build new knowledge based on their intuitive knowledge and informal procedures. Students learn both concepts and skills by solving problems (Cobb, 1991).

• It stimulates whole-class discussion following individual and group work. In addition to promoting communication, this serves as an effective diagnostic tool. Research suggests that teachers should provide opportunities such as activities, problems, and assignments for students to interact (i.e., work in small groups and share ideas) in problem-rich situations (Davidson, 1985).

More Research to Support the Use of Math Test Prep That Matters!

• Teaching math with a focus on number sense encourages students to become problem solvers in a wide variety of situations and to view mathematics as a discipline that is important (Markovits & Sowder, 1994; Cobb, 1991).

- Long-term use of concrete materials is positively related to increases in student mathematics achievement and improved attitudes towards mathematics (Suydam & Higgins, 1977; Driscoll, 1990). In a recent meta-analysis of sixty studies (kindergarten through post-secondary) that compared the effects of using concrete materials with the effects of more abstract instruction, Sowell (1989) found that long-term use of concrete materials by teachers knowledgeable in their use improved student achievement and attitudes. John van de Walle's translation model demonstrates how we can develop understanding from one external representation of an idea to another (van de Walle, 1998; Lesh, Post, & Behr, 1987).

- Numerous studies of mathematics achievement at different grade and ability levels show that students benefit when real objects (manipulatives) are used as aids in learning mathematics (Bennett, 1986).

- *EDThoughts: What We Know About Mathematics Teaching and Learning* offers numerous citings related to effective instructional methods where time is allotted for students to individually ponder appropriate strategies; identify necessary tools to assist in solving the problem; work in small groups exploring and discussing ideas and solving the problem; and report their findings to the class (Sutton, 2002).

How to Use This Book

The standards-based prompts in this book are arranged by the content and process strands typically found in an NCTM standards-based curriculum. The prompts feature graphics similar to those in student texts and on formative and normative assessments, further supporting the alignment of standards, assessment, and instruction. Offer these graphic prompts only after you have instructed students on the basic concepts using practices that include hands-on/concrete manipulatives, models, and representations (Sowell, 1989).

The graphic prompts are designed so that students can easily recognize the content area highlighted and then develop a written and/or oral response to the graphic. This strategy helps build students' content knowledge (conceptual understanding and their related skills) while developing and strengthening their process skills (i.e., problem solving, reasoning and proof, oral and written communication, connections, and representation). The graphic prompts across all content and process strands are designed to promote thinking, reasoning, problem solving, and oral and written communication (Sutton, 2002).

After students have shared their responses to a graphic prompt, you may wish to offer a challenge or extension related to the same prompt. Embedded assessment helps you determine a student's level of understanding of content based upon his or her responses. Following are some examples of how you can use the graphic prompts to assess students' learning and further challenge them:

Number and Operations

Page 16: Students should recognize the base-ten model for 42. They might ask a simple math question, like: *What is one more (or ten more or comes just before) 42?* (Notice how asking a math question promotes use of mathematical language.) Students then answer their own question, saying: *Ten more than 42 is 52.* As an extension, challenge students to model the number 42 in two other ways.

Page 21: Students should recognize 6 as the symbol for the word and as a cardinal number. A more advanced student might ask: *How would you show the repeated addition (or the basic fact for multiplication) for the model shown? (The repeated addition is 2 + 2 + 2 = 6 [or the basic fact in multiplication is 3 x 2 = 6]).* Challenge students to model 2 x 5 = 10 or to show the principle of commutativity (5 x 2 = 10).

Algebra

Page 29: Expect students to understand the pattern and extend it. An obvious question they might ask is: *What are the next three letters in the pattern? (G, B, and G)* Challenge students to extend the pattern further and identify the 12th or 15th child in the pattern.

Page 32: More advanced students might recognize the circles as addends, each with a value of 2, and then proceed to discover and explain the value of the star (3) and the squares (4). A logical question would then be: *What is the value of the hexagon? (6)* Invite students to create a similar 3 x 3 grid or even a 4 x 4 grid.

Geometry

Page 33: In this activity, students use mathematical language to explain what they see. A typical question might be: *How are the shapes and figures the same? (They are all plane.) How are they different? (Three are quadrilaterals, while the circle is not.)* As an extension, encourage students to create a 2 x 2 grid that shows solids.

Measurement

Page 40: Looking at the graphic, students should infer that the weight of the cubes is equal to the weight of the spheres. Students might ask: *What is the weight of each cube and sphere? (Each cube weighs 3 ounces and each sphere weighs 2 ounces.)* Challenge students to calculate other possible weights for the cubes and spheres and still have them balance.

Data Analysis and Probability

Page 52: After writing about what they see, students might ask: *If I reach in and pick a shape, which am I more likely to pick? (It is more likely that I will pick a star. It is less likely that I will pick a square. It is impossible to reach in and pick a circle.)* Challenge students to calculate the probability of reaching in and picking a star or a square.

Problem Solving

Page 54: In this activity, students explore and write about shapes and figures they can create using sticks. After filling in the charts, they might ask: *How many hexagons can be created with 24 sticks? (4)* Pose this challenge: *A student used all 24 sticks to make three different shapes. How many of each shape did she make?* (HINT: There was at least one hexagon, one triangle, and one square).

Reasoning and Proof

Page 56: Guide students to describe the task—use mathematics language to describe the shapes and the parts of the triangle. Make sure students understand the problem by having them restate it in their own words. Ask: *Which problem-solving strategy would you use to solve the problem? (Guess and check)* Possible solution: Starting at one angle of the triangle, place these numbers in order clockwise: 1, 6, 2, 4, 3, 5, 1. Each side will add up to 9. (Other solutions have each side adding up to 10, 11, or 12.) For an additional challenge, have students draw a 3 x 3 grid and place the digits 1 through 9 in the boxes so that they add up to 15 vertically, horizontally, and diagonally.

Communication

Page 59: After writing about what they see, students might ask: *About how many marbles are there in jar A? (50)* Challenge students to estimate how many marbles there are in all three jars.

Connections

Page 61: After students have completed their Numbers All Around Me sheet, encourage them to compare their addresses with one another; for example, noting whether their address is odd or even. As an extension, study maps of your town or city to identify zip codes. Possible discussion topics could include: Why do the postal authorities encourage us to use four additional digits with our zip code? Compare your telephone area code with your classmates'.

Representation

Page 62: This model is recommended for developing the concept of the missing addend when teaching the different models for subtraction: (a) take away; (b) comparison; (c) the missing addend. Guide students to notice that all of her dogs are not in the yard; some are in the doghouse. You may want to create models to represent the problem. For example, 3 + [doghouse] = 5. A typical question would be: *How many dogs are in the doghouse? (2)* Encourage students to create problems (algorithms) and use models or representations; for example, an owner has seven dogs and three are in the doghouse.

Bibliography

Resources for Developing, Supporting, and Strengthening Mathematical Proficiency

Bennett, W. J. (1986). *What works: Research about teaching and learning.* Washington, DC: United States Department of Education.

Broad Prize for Urban Education. (2002). *Showcasing success/Rewarding achievement.* Austin, TX: National Center for Educational Accountability.

Brownell, W. A. (1945). When is arithmetic meaningful? *Journal of Education Research, 38,* 481–498.

Clements, D. H., Sarama, J., & DiBiase, A.-M. (Eds.). (2004). *Engaging young children in mathematics: Standards for early childhood mathematics education.* Mahwah, NJ: Erlbaum.

Cobb, P. et al. (1991). Assessment of a problem-centered second-grade mathematics project. *Journal for Research in Mathematics Education, 22,* 3–29.

Davidson, N. (1985). Small-group cooperative learning in mathematics: A selective view of the research. In R. Hertz-Lazarowitz, S. Kagan, S. Sharan, R. Slavin, & C. Webb (Eds.), *Learning to Cooperate, Cooperating to Learn* (pp. 211–230). New York: Plenum.

Driscoll, M. J. (1982). *Research within reach: Elementary school mathematics.* Reston, VA: National Council of Teachers of Mathematics.

Driscoll, M. J. (1990). The teacher's role: Manipulatives from The bridge from concrete to abstract. In M. J. Driscoll, *Research within reach: Elementary school mathematics* (6th printing). Reston, VA: National Council of Teachers of Mathematics.

Friedman, T. L. (2005). *The world is flat: A brief history of the twenty-first century.* New York: Farrar, Straus & Giroux.

GOALS 2000: Educate America Act. (1994, March 31). Pub. Law 103-227 (108 Stat.125)

Kilpatrick, J., Swafford, J., & Findell, B. (Eds.). (2001). *Adding it up: Helping children learn mathematics.* Washington, DC: National Academy Press.

Lesh, R. A., Post, T. R., & Behr, M. J. (1987). Representations and translations among representations in mathematics learning and problem solving." In C. Janvier (Ed.), *Problems of representation in the teaching and learning of mathematics* (pp. 33–40). Hillsdale, NJ: Erlbaum.

Markovits, Z., & Sowder, J. (1994). Developing number sense: An intervention study in grade 7. *Journal for Research in Mathematics Education, 25,* 4–29.

National Research Council. (1989). *Everybody counts: A report to the nation on the future of mathematics education.* Washington, DC: National Academies Press

National Assessment of Educational Progress (NAEP). National Center for Educational Statistics. Institute of Educational Sciences. United States Department of Education. http://nces.ed.gov/nationsreportcard/

National Commission of Excellence in Education. (1983). *A nation at risk: The imperative for educational reform.* Washington, DC: U.S. Government Printing Office.

New York State Education Department. (2005, March). *Mathematics core curriculum.* http://www.emsc.nysed.gov /ciai/mst/mathstandards/revised3.htm

Principles and standards for school mathematics. (2000). Reston, VA: National Council of Teachers of Mathematics.

Solomon, P. G. (2000). *The math we need to "know" and "do": Content standards for elementary and middle grades.* Thousand Oaks, CA: Corwin Press.

Sowell, E. J. (1989). Effects of manipulative materials in mathematics instruction. *Journal for Research in Mathematics Education, 20,* 409–505.

Stenmark, J. K. (Ed.). (1991). *Mathematics assessment: Myths, models, good questions and practical suggestions.* Reston, VA: National Council of Teachers of Mathematics.

Sutton, J., & Krueger, A. (Eds.). (2002). *EDThoughts: What we know about mathematics teaching and learning.* Aurora: CO: Mid-Continental Research for Education and Learning.

Suydam, M. N., & Higgins, J. L. (1977). *Activity-based learning in elementary school mathematics: Recommendations from research.* Columbus, OH: ERIC/Clearinghouse for Science, Mathematics, and Environmental Education.

Trends in International Mathematics and Science Study. International Association for the Evaluation of Educational Achievement. U.S. Department of Education. http://nces.ed.gov/timss/

Van de Walle, J. A. (1998). *Elementary and middle school mathematics: Teaching developmentally* (3rd ed.). New York: Addison Wesley Longman.

NCTM Standards

Standard – Instructional programs from Pre-kindergarten through Grade 12 should enable all students to:	Expectations – In Pre-kindergarten through Grade 2, all students should:
I: Number and Operations	
A. Understand numbers, ways of representing numbers, relationships among numbers, and number systems	**1.** Count with understanding and recognize "how many" in sets of objects; **2.** Use multiple models to develop initial understandings of place value and the base-ten number system; **3.** Develop understanding of the relative position and magnitude of whole numbers and of ordinal numbers and cardinal numbers and their connections; **4.** Develop a sense of whole numbers and represent and use them in flexible ways, including relating, composing, and decomposing numbers; **5.** Connect number words and numerals to the quantities they represent, using various physical models and representations; **6.** Understand and represent commonly used fractions, such as $\frac{1}{4}$, $\frac{1}{3}$, and $\frac{1}{2}$.
B. Understand meanings of operations and how they relate to one another	**1.** Understand various meanings of addition and subtraction of whole numbers and the relationship between the two operations; **2.** Understand the effects of adding and subtracting whole numbers; **3.** Understand situations that entail multiplication and division, such as equal groupings of objects and sharing equally.
C. Compute fluently and make reasonable estimates	**1.** Develop and use strategies for whole number computations, with a focus on addition and subtraction; **2.** Develop fluency with basic number combinations for addition and subtraction; **3.** Use a variety of methods and tools to compute, including objects, mental computation, estimation, paper and pencil, and calculators.
II. Algebra	
A. Understand patterns, relations, and functions	**1.** Sort, classify, and order objects by size, number, and other properties; **2.** Recognize, describe, and extend patterns such as sequences of sounds and shapes or simple numeric patterns and translate from one representation to another; **3.** Analyze how both repeating and growing patterns are generated.
B. Represent and analyze mathematical situations and structures using algebraic symbols	**1.** Illustrate general principles and properties of operations, such as commutativity, using specific numbers; **2.** Use concrete, pictorial, and verbal representations to develop an understanding of invented and conventional symbolic notations.
C. Use mathematical models to represent and understand quantitative relationships	**1.** Model situations that involve the addition and subtraction of whole numbers, using objects, pictures, and symbols.
D. Analyze change in various contexts	**1.** Describe qualitative change, such as a student's growing taller; **2.** Describe quantitative change, such as a student's growing two inches in one year.
III. Geometry	
A. Analyze characteristics and properties of two- and three-dimensional geometric shapes and develop mathematical arguments about geometric relationships	**1.** Recognize, name, build, draw, compare, and sort two- and three-dimensional shapes; **2.** Describe attributes and parts of two- and three-dimensional shapes; **3.** Investigate and predict the results of putting together and taking apart two- and three-dimensional shapes.

Standard – Instructional programs from Pre-kindergarten through Grade 12 should enable all students to:	Expectations – In Pre-kindergarten through Grade 2, all students should:	
B. Specify locations and describe spatial relationships using coordinate geometry and other representational systems	1. Describe, name, and interpret relative positions in space and apply ideas about relative position; 2. Describe, name, and interpret direction and distance in navigating space and apply ideas about direction and distance; 3. Find and name locations with simple relationships such as "near to" and in coordinate systems such as maps.	III. Geometry
C. Apply transformations and use symmetry to analyze mathematical situations	1. Recognize and apply slides, flips, and turns; 2. Recognize and create shapes that have symmetry.	
D. Use visualization, spatial reasoning, and geometric modeling to solve problems	1. Create mental images of geometric shapes using spatial memory and spatial visualization; 2. Recognize and represent shapes from different perspectives; 3. Relate ideas in geometry to ideas in number and measurement; 4. Recognize geometric shapes and structures in the environment and specify their location.	
A. Understand measurable attributes of objects and the units, systems, and processes of measurement	1. Recognize the attributes of length, volume, weight, area, and time; 2. Compare and order objects according to these attributes; 3. Understand how to measure using nonstandard and standard units; 4. Select an appropriate unit and tool for the attribute being measured.	IV. Measurement
B. Apply appropriate techniques, tools, and formulas to determine measurements	1. Measure with multiple copies of units of the same size, such as paper clips laid end to end; 2. Use repetition of a single unit to measure something larger than the unit, for instance, measuring the length of a room with a single meterstick; 3. Use tools to measure; 4. Develop common referents for measures to make comparisons and estimates.	
A. Formulate questions that can be addressed with data and collect, organize, and display relevant data to answer them	1. Pose questions and gather data about themselves and their surroundings; 2. Sort and classify objects according to their attributes and organize data about the objects; 3. Represent data using concrete objects, pictures, and graphs.	V. Data Analysis and Probability
B. Select and use appropriate statistical methods to analyze data	1. Describe parts of the data and the set of data as a whole to determine what the data show.	
C. Develop and evaluate inferences and predictions that are based on data	1. Discuss events related to students' experiences as likely or unlikely.	
D. Understand and apply basic concepts of probability		

	Standard – Instructional programs from Pre-kindergarten through Grade 12 should enable all students to:
VI. Problem Solving	**A.** Build new mathematical knowledge through problem solving;
	B. Solve problems that arise in mathematics and in other contexts;
	C. Apply and adapt a variety of appropriate strategies to solve problems;
	D. Monitor and reflect on the process of mathematical problem solving.
VII. Reasoning and Proof	**A.** Recognize reasoning and proof as fundamental aspects of mathematics;
	B. Make and investigate mathematical conjectures;
	C. Develop and evaluate mathematical arguments and proofs;
	D. Select and use various types of reasoning and methods of proof.
VIII. Communication	**A.** Organize and consolidate their mathematical thinking through communication;
	B. Communicate their mathematical thinking coherently and clearly to peers, teachers, and others;
	C. Analyze and evaluate the mathematical thinking and strategies of others;
	D. Use the language of mathematics to express mathematical ideas precisely.
IX. Connections	**A.** Recognize and use connections among mathematical ideas;
	B. Understand how mathematical ideas interconnect and build on one another to produce a coherent whole;
	C. Recognize and apply mathematics in contexts outside of mathematics.
X. Representation	**A.** Create and use representations to organize, record, and communicate mathematical ideas;
	B. Select, apply, and translate among mathematical representations to solve problems;
	C. Use representations to model and interpret physical, social, and mathematical phenomena.

* Standards notation on activity pages:
  S: I A / E: 1 means the activity meets the Number & Operations (I)
  Standard A (Understand numbers, ways of representing numbers, . . .),
  Expectation 1 (Count with understanding . . .).

Name: _____ Date: _____

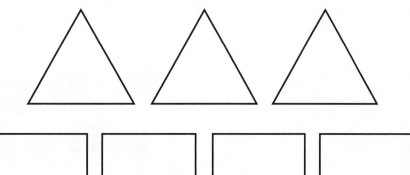

1. Write about what you see above.

_____

_____

_____

2. Ask a math question about it.

_____

_____

_____

3. Answer your question.

_____

_____

_____

Math Test Prep That Matters! Grades K–2   Scholastic Teaching Resources

S: I A / E: 1

Name: _____ Date: _____

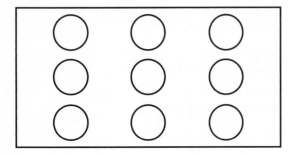 

1. Write about what you see above.

_____

_____

_____

2. Ask a math question about it.

_____

_____

_____

3. Answer your question.

_____

_____

_____

Name: _____ Date: _____

Tens	Ones

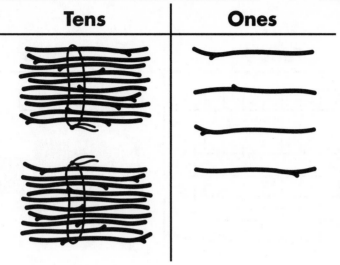

1. Write about what you see above.

_____

_____

_____

2. Ask a math question about it.

_____

_____

_____

3. Answer your question.

_____

_____

_____

Math Test Prep That Matters! Grades K–2   Scholastic Teaching Resources

Name: _____ Date: _____

Tens	Ones
□□□□□□□□□□ □□□□□□□□□□ □□□□□□□□□□ □□□□□□□□□□	□ □

1. Write about what you see above.

_____

_____

_____

2. Ask a math question about it.

_____

_____

_____

3. Answer your question.

_____

_____

_____

S: I A / E: 2

Math Test Prep That Matters! Grades K–2   Scholastic Teaching Resources

Name: _____ Date: _____

A	B
243	**2 hundreds** **4 tens** **3 ones**
C	D
200 + 40 + 3	Hundreds Tens Ones

1. Write about what you see above.

_____

_____

_____

2. Ask a math question about it.

_____

_____

_____

3. Answer your question.

_____

_____

_____

Math Test Prep That Matters! Grades K–2   Scholastic Teaching Resources

17

S: I A / E: 2

Name: _____ Date: _____

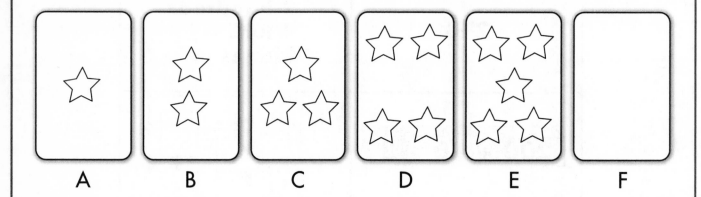

A   B   C   D   E   F

1. Write about what you see above.

_____

_____

_____

2. Ask a math question about it.

_____

_____

_____

3. Answer your question.

_____

_____

_____

Math Test Prep That Matters! Grades K–2   Scholastic Teaching Resources

S: I A / E: 3

Name: _____ Date: _____

1. Write about what you see above.

_____

_____

_____

2. Ask a math question about it.

_____

_____

_____

3. Answer your question.

_____

_____

_____

S: I A / E: 4

Name: _____   Date: _____

A. ☐☐☐☐☐☐	6 + 0 = 6	
B. ☐☐☐☐☐■	5 + 1 = 6	
C. ☐☐☐☐■■	4 + 2 = 6	
D. ☐☐☐■■■	3 + 3 = 6	
E. ☐☐■■■■	_____	
F. ☐■■■■■	_____	
G. ■■■■■■	_____	

1. Write about what you see above.

_____

_____

_____

2. Ask a math question about it.

_____

_____

_____

3. Answer your question.

_____

_____

_____

Math Test Prep That Matters! Grades K–2   Scholastic Teaching Resources

S: I A / E: 4

Name: _____   Date: _____

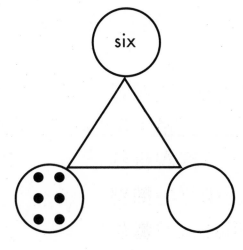

1. Write about what you see above.

_____

_____

_____

2. Ask a math question about it.

_____

_____

_____

3. Answer your question.

_____

_____

_____

Name: _____ Date: _____

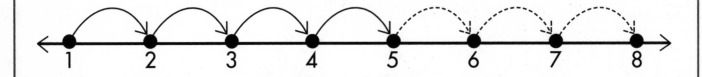

1. Write about what you see above.

_____

_____

_____

2. Ask a math question about it.

_____

_____

_____

3. Answer your question.

_____

_____

_____

Math Test Prep That Matters! Grades K–2   Scholastic Teaching Resources

S: I C / E: 1

Name: _____ Date: _____

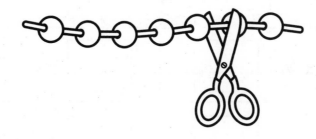

1. Write about what you see above.

_____

_____

_____

2. Ask a math question about it.

_____

_____

_____

3. Answer your question.

_____

_____

_____

Math Test Prep That Matters! Grades K–2 Scholastic Teaching Resources

23

S: I B / E: 1, 2

Name: _____ Date: _____

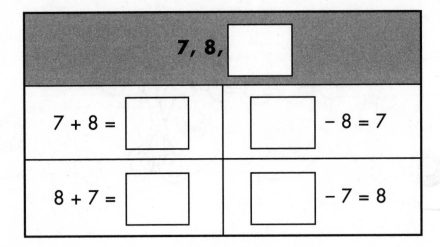

1. Write about what you see above.

_____

_____

_____

2. Ask a math question about it.

_____

_____

_____

3. Answer your question.

_____

_____

_____

S: I B / E: 1

Math Test Prep That Matters! Grades K–2 Scholastic Teaching Resources

Name: _____ Date: _____

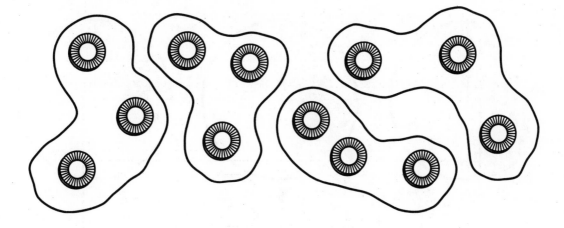

1. Write about what you see above.

_____

_____

_____

2. Ask a math question about it.

_____

_____

_____

3. Answer your question.

_____

_____

_____

S: I B / E: 3

Name: _____   Date: _____

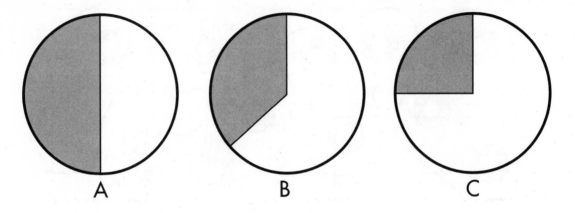

1. Write about what you see above.

_____

_____

_____

2. Ask a math question about it.

_____

_____

_____

3. Answer your question.

_____

_____

_____

S: I A / E: 6

Math Test Prep That Matters! Grades K–2   Scholastic Teaching Resources

Name: _____   Date: _____

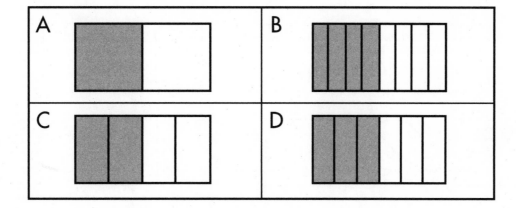

1. Write about what you see above.

_____

_____

_____

2. Ask a math question about it.

_____

_____

_____

3. Answer your question.

_____

_____

_____

Math Test Prep That Matters! Grades K–2   Scholastic Teaching Resources

S: I A / E: 6

Name: _____   Date: _____

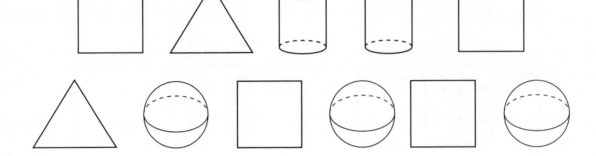

1. Write about what you see above.

_____

_____

_____

2. Ask a math question about it.

_____

_____

_____

3. Answer your question.

_____

_____

_____

Algebra

S: II A / E: 1

Math Test Prep That Matters! Grades K–2 Scholastic Teaching Resources

Name: _____   Date: _____

B   G   G   B   G   G   B   G   _____   _____

1. Write about what you see above.

_____

_____

_____

2. Ask a math question about it.

_____

_____

_____

3. Answer your question.

_____

_____

_____

Math Test Prep That Matters! Grades K–2   Scholastic Teaching Resources

29

S: II A / E: 2

Name: _____ Date: _____

Number of pencils	Cost of pencils
1	10 cents
2	20 cents
3	30 cents
4	
5	

1. Write about what you see above.

_____

_____

_____

2. Ask a math question about it.

_____

_____

_____

3. Answer your question.

_____

_____

_____

Name: _____ Date: _____

In September, I was 47 inches tall. Now in June, I am one inch *more* than four feet.

1. Write about what you see above.

_____

_____

_____

2. Ask a math question about it.

_____

_____

_____

3. Answer your question.

_____

_____

_____

Math Test Prep That Matters! Grades K–2   Scholastic Teaching Resources

31

S: II D / E: 1, 2

Name: _____   Date: _____

Hint:
The shapes
are addends.

			Sum
□	□	○	10
○	○	○	6
⬡	△	☆	14
Sum 12	11	7	

1. Write about what you see above.

_____

_____

_____

2. Ask a math question about it.

_____

_____

_____

3. Answer your question.

_____

_____

_____

Math Test Prep That Matters! Grades K–2   Scholastic Teaching Resources

S: II C/ E: 1

Name: _____ Date: _____

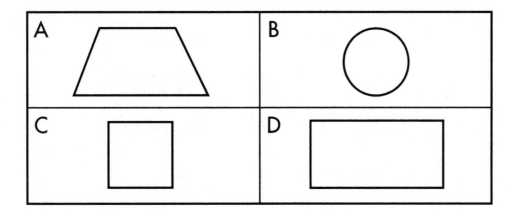

1. Write about what you see above.

_____

_____

_____

2. Ask a math question about it.

_____

_____

_____

3. Answer your question.

_____

_____

_____

Math Test Prep That Matters! Grades K–2   Scholastic Teaching Resources

33

S: III A / E: 1

Name: _____ Date: _____

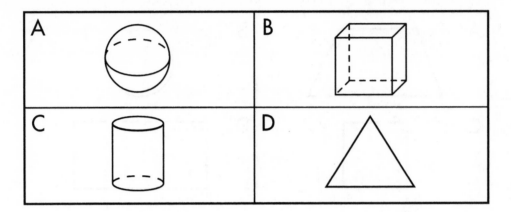

1. Write about what you see above.

_____

_____

_____

2. Ask a math question about it.

_____

_____

_____

3. Answer your question.

_____

_____

_____

S: III A / E: 2

Math Test Prep That Matters! Grades K–2   Scholastic Teaching Resources

Name: _____ Date: _____

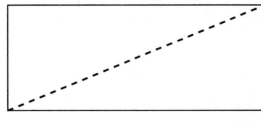
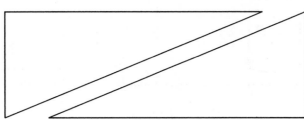

1. Write about what you see above.

_____

_____

_____

2. Ask a math question about it.

_____

_____

_____

3. Answer your question.

_____

_____

_____

S: III A / E: 3

Name: _____ Date: _____

My Neighborhood

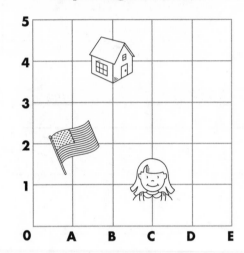

1. Write about what you see above.

_____

_____

_____

2. Ask a math question about it.

_____

_____

_____

3. Answer your question.

_____

_____

_____

Name: _____ Date: _____

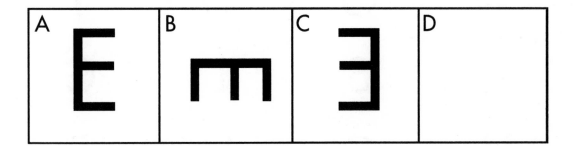

1. Write about what you see above.

_____

_____

_____

2. Ask a math question about it.

_____

_____

_____

3. Answer your question.

_____

_____

_____

S: III C / E: 1

Name: _____ Date: _____

A   O   W   T

R   S   L   G

H   Q   M   R

1. Write about what you see above.

_____

_____

_____

2. Ask a math question about it.

_____

_____

_____

3. Answer your question.

_____

_____

_____

Math Test Prep That Matters! Grades K–2 Scholastic Teaching Resources

S: III C / E: 2

Name: _____ Date: _____

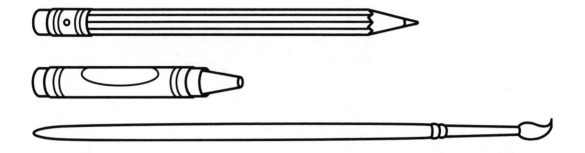

1. Write about what you see above.

_____

_____

_____

2. Ask a math question about it.

_____

_____

_____

3. Answer your question.

_____

_____

_____

S: IV A / E: 1

Name: _____ Date: _____

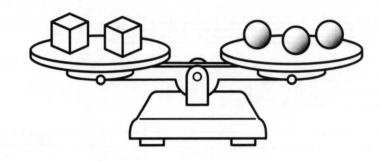

1. Write about what you see above.

_____

_____

_____

2. Ask a math question about it.

_____

_____

_____

3. Answer your question.

_____

_____

_____

Math Test Prep That Matters! Grades K–2 Scholastic Teaching Resources

Name: _____   Date: _____

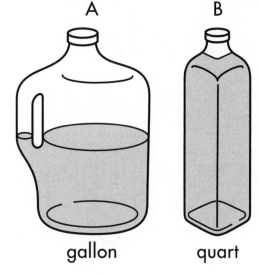

A
gallon

B
quart

1. Write about what you see above.

_____

_____

_____

2. Ask a math question about it.

_____

_____

_____

3. Answer your question.

_____

_____

_____

S: IV A / E: 3

Name: _____ Date: _____

1. Write about what you see above.

_____

_____

_____

2. Ask a math question about it.

_____

_____

_____

3. Answer your question.

_____

_____

_____

S: IV A / E: 3, 4

Math Test Prep That Matters! Grades K–2   Scholastic Teaching Resources

Name: _____ Date: _____

1. Write about what you see above.

_____

_____

_____

2. Ask a math question about it.

_____

_____

_____

3. Answer your question.

_____

_____

_____

S: IV A / E: 3, 4

Name: _____   Date: _____

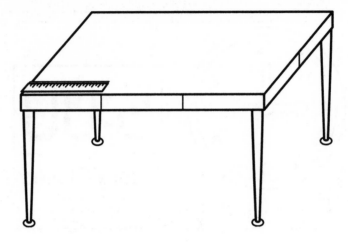

1. Write about what you see above.

_____

_____

_____

2. Ask a math question about it.

_____

_____

_____

3. Answer your question.

_____

_____

_____

S: IV B / E: 2, 3, 4

Name: _____ Date: _____

1. Write about what you see above.

_____

_____

_____

2. Ask a math question about it.

_____

_____

_____

3. Answer your question.

_____

_____

_____

S: IV B / E: 1

Name: _____   Date: _____

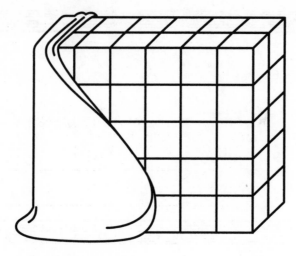

1. Write about what you see above.

_____

_____

_____

2. Ask a math question about it.

_____

_____

_____

3. Answer your question.

_____

_____

_____

Math Test Prep That Matters! Grades K–2   Scholastic Teaching Resources

S: IV B / E: 4

Name: _____   Date: _____

Shapes	Tally Marks
Circles	~~IIII~~ I
Squares	II
Triangles	

1. Write about what you see above.

_____

_____

_____

2. Ask a math question about it.

_____

_____

_____

3. Answer your question.

_____

_____

_____

Math Test Prep That Matters! Grades K–2   Scholastic Teaching Resources

47

S: V A / E: 2

Name: _____   Date: _____

Favorite Flavors of Ice Cream

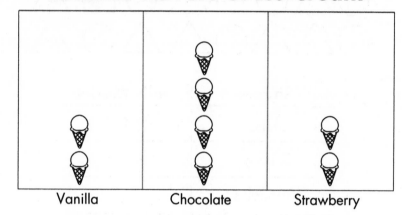

Vanilla   Chocolate   Strawberry

1. Write about what you see above.

_____

_____

_____

2. Ask a math question about it.

_____

_____

_____

3. Answer your question.

_____

_____

_____

S: V A / E: 1, 3

Name: _____ Date: _____

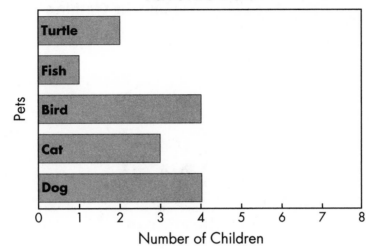

Favorite Pets

1. Write about what you see above.

_____

_____

_____

2. Ask a math question about it.

_____

_____

_____

3. Answer your question.

_____

_____

_____

Math Test Prep That Matters! Grades K–2   Scholastic Teaching Resources

S: V A / E: 1, 3

Name: _____ Date: _____

Number of Buttons on Our Clothing

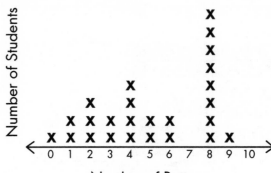

1. Write about what you see above.

_____

_____

_____

2. Ask a math question about it.

_____

_____

_____

3. Answer your question.

_____

_____

_____

S: V A / E: 1, 3

Math Test Prep That Matters! Grades K–2   Scholastic Teaching Resources

Name: _____   Date: _____

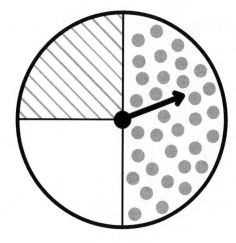

1. Write about what you see above.

_____

_____

_____

2. Ask a math question about it.

_____

_____

_____

3. Answer your question.

_____

_____

_____

Math Test Prep That Matters! Grades K–2   Scholastic Teaching Resources

51

S: V D

Name: _____ Date: _____

 ____ likely ____

____ less likely

____ impossible

1. Write about what you see above.

_____

_____

_____

2. Ask a math question about it.

_____

_____

_____

3. Answer your question.

_____

_____

_____

S: V C / E: 1

Math Test Prep That Matters! Grades K–2   Scholastic Teaching Resources

Name: _____ Date: _____

Quarters	Dimes	Nickels	Pennies	Total
1	0	0	1	26¢
0	2	1	1	26¢
				26¢
				26¢

1. Write about what you see above.

_____

_____

_____

2. Ask a math question about it.

_____

_____

_____

3. Answer your question.

_____

_____

_____

S: VI B, C, D

Name: _____ Date: _____

24 STICKS

Triangles	1	2	3					
Number of Sticks	3	6						

Squares	1	2	3			
Number of Sticks	4	8				

1. Write about what you see above.

_____

_____

_____

2. Ask a math question about it.

_____

_____

_____

3. Answer your question.

_____

_____

_____

S: VI A, C

Name: _____ Date: _____

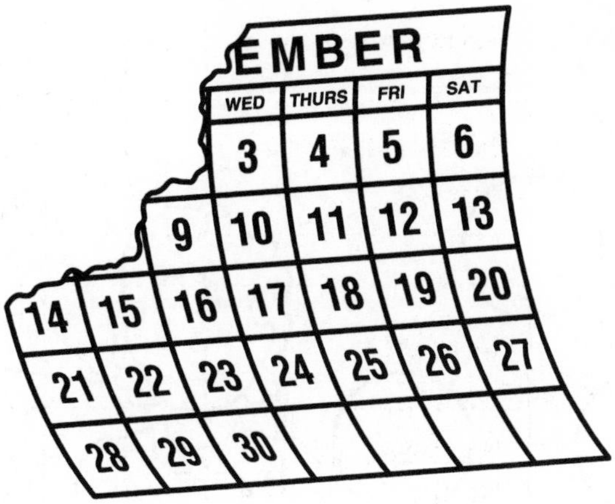

1. Write about what you see above.

_____

_____

_____

2. Ask a math question about it.

_____

_____

_____

3. Answer your question.

_____

_____

_____

S: VI C, D

Name: _____ Date: _____

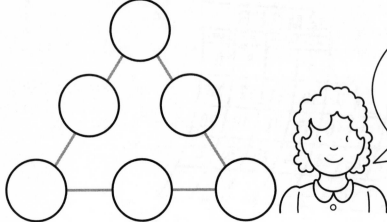

Place the numbers 1 to 6 in the circles. Can you make each side of the triangle add up to the same sum?

1. Write about what you see above.

_____

_____

_____

2. Ask a math question about it.

_____

_____

_____

3. Answer your question.

_____

_____

_____

Math Test Prep That Matters! Grades K–2 Scholastic Teaching Resources

S: VII A, B, C, D

Name: _____ Date: _____

Pet	Number of Legs	Number of Pets
Birds		
Dogs		
Total	18	

At the pet shop, I counted 18 legs. How many dogs and birds did I see?

1. Write about what you see above.

_____

_____

_____

2. Ask a math question about it.

_____

_____

_____

3. Answer your question.

_____

_____

_____

Math Test Prep That Matters! Grades K–2 Scholastic Teaching Resources

S: VII A, B, C, D

Name: _____ Date: _____

1. Write about what you see above.

_____

_____

_____

2. Ask a math question about it.

_____

_____

_____

3. Answer your question.

_____

_____

_____

S: VIII A, B, C, D

Name: _____ Date: _____

My jar has 100 marbles.

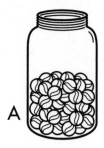

A

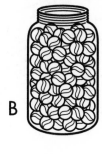

B

C

1. Write about what you see above.

_____

_____

_____

2. Ask a math question about it.

_____

_____

_____

3. Answer your question.

_____

_____

_____

S: VIII A, B, C, D

Name: _____ Date: _____

1. Write about what you see above.

_____

_____

_____

2. Ask a math question about it.

_____

_____

_____

3. Answer your question.

_____

_____

_____

S: IX A, B, C

Name: _____ Date: _____

Numbers All Around Me

Address: _____

Zip Code: _____

Telephone Number: _____

Bus Number: _____

1. Write about what you see above.

_____

_____

_____

2. Ask a math question about it.

_____

_____

_____

3. Answer your question.

_____

_____

_____

Name: _____ Date: _____

1. Write about what you see above.

_____

_____

_____

2. Ask a math question about it.

_____

_____

_____

3. Answer your question.

_____

_____

_____

S: X A, B, C

Math Test Prep That Matters! Grades K–2 Scholastic Teaching Resources

Name: _____ Date: _____

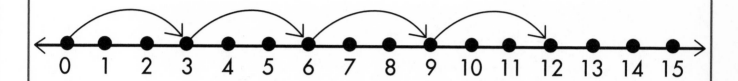

1. Write about what you see above.

_____

_____

_____

2. Ask a math question about it.

_____

_____

_____

3. Answer your question.

_____

_____

_____

Math Test Prep That Matters! Grades K–2   Scholastic Teaching Resources

63

S: X A, B, C

Name: _____ Date: _____

1. Write about what you see above.

_____

_____

_____

2. Ask a math question about it.

_____

_____

_____

3. Answer your question.

_____

_____

_____